CW01190854

CATS REACT to OUTER SPACE FACTS

By Izzi Howell

WAYLAND
www.waylandbooks.co.uk

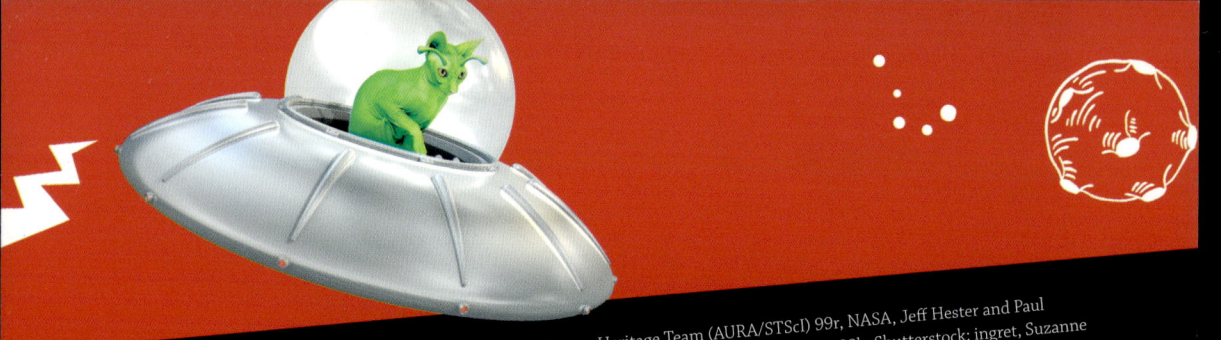

First published in Great Britain in 2020 by Wayland
Copyright © Hodder and Stoughton Limited, 2020

All rights reserved.

ISBN: 978 1 5263 1341 6 (HB)
      978 1 5263 1342 3 (PB)

Produced for Wayland by
White-Thomson Publishing Ltd
www.wtpub.co.uk

Editor: Izzi Howell and Paul Rockett
Designer: Clare Nicholas

Printed in China

Wayland
An imprint of
Hachette Children's Group
Part of Hodder & Stoughton
Carmelite House
50 Victoria Embankment
London EC4Y 0DZ

An Hachette UK Company
www.hachette.co.uk
www.hachettechildrens.co.uk

MIX
Paper from
responsible sources
FSC® C104740

The publisher would like to thank the following for permission to reproduce their pictures:

Alamy: MARK GARLICK/SCIENCE PHOTO LIBRARY 15; ESA/DLR/FU Berlin/BY-SA 3.0 IGO: 37; Getty: ZargonDesign 2t, bahadir-yeniceri 5, lynnebeclu 20, Beboy_ltd 27t, goir 29, iridi 38b, PaulFleet 40, 3quarks 46–47, GlobalP 50l, spxChrome 54, NikShargin 55t, solarseven 62r, aryos 65, lepas2004 and ghoststone 66–67, Viorika 69, adogslifephoto 73, frentusha 87, iridi 88t, Игорь Салов 89, funebre 91, Shenki 92, Devrimb 96, jamesbenet 98, murayann 100, phant 101, lepas2004 112; NASA: ESA/Hubble 64l, ESA/NASA 68l, NASA 73, 94 and 100, NASA/JPL-Caltech/R. Hurt (SSC/Caltech) 74r, NASA's Goddard Space Flight Center 83t, ESO/M. Kornmesser 84, NASA and The Hubble Heritage Team (STScI/AURA); Acknowledgment: Ray A. Lucas (STScI/AURA) 85t, NASA and The Hubble Heritage Team (AURA/STScI) 99r, NASA, Jeff Hester and Paul Scowen Arizona State University 99b; Shutterstock: ingret, Suzanne Tucker, Valentina Razumova, Evgeny Karandaev, Kwanbenz back cover, ingret cover, Missarabika title page, Sergey Moskvitin 2t, aquariagirl1970 2b and 13, 3D Vector 3t, Tuzemka 3b, kuban_girl and Tom Wang 4t, stockphoto-graf 4b, umnola 5, Withan Tor 6–7c, Dora Zett 7t and 109t, Andrey_Kuzmin and Nasky 7b, eddtoro 8t, Iryna Kuznetsova 8b, 15, 20, 22, 33, 37, 61b, 72, 87 and 102b, Pakhnyushchy 9, Levchenko Ilia 10t, DenisNata 10b, NikoNomad and Lady Shmidt-Studio 11 and 109b, Andrey_Kuzmin 12t, 20 and 42, Designua 12b, Tuzemka 13, Alexey Repka 14t, Sari Oneal 14b, Mopic 16t, Ermolaev Alexander 16b, 20, 37, 45 and 85l, Kasefoto, Bborriss.67 and Waqar Ahmed 86 17, Puwadol Jaturawutthichai and claire Bullion 18, Vladyslav Starozhylov 19, Tsekhmister and Tasha Drik 20, Dotted Yeti and Tony Campbell 21, NASA images and Nerthuz 22, DK samco 23t, Castleski 23b, Arkadi Bulva and esfera 24t, Kasefoto and Vadim Sadovski 24b, Nerthuz 25t, kuban_girl 25b, 44 and 86r, Phanuwat Yoksiri 26, Eric Isselee 27b, 29 77, 79 and 105, YummyBuum 28t, FotoYakov 28b, Mega Pixel, Photoonlife, HK-PHOTOGRAPHY 29, night_cat 31, Robynrg 32t, Vadim Sadovski 32b and 56t, Rachel Juliet Lerch 34, Olesya Baron 35, Martina Osmy 36l, Triff 36r, Alexeysun and Nattika 38t, Luciano Mortula – LGM 39, andrea crisante 40, Happy monkey 41l, Vadim Sadovski 41r, 44, 52, 60l and 86l Dotted Yeti 43t, Sergey Nivens and Sonsedska Yuliia 43b, turlakova and Sonsedska Yuliia 44, Grigorita Ko, BravissimoS and PRILL 46–47, Natee Jitthammachai 48t, nevodka and Ian 2010 48b, Susan Schmitz 49, NASA images 50r and 55b, Angela Kotsell and ComicSans 51, Seregraff 52, Oleksandr Lytvynenko 53, diversepixel and vvvita 54, Krasowit 56b, Tony Campbell 57l, 78 and 92, Kasefoto and Sergiy1975 57r, SV_zt, Robynrg, Linn Currie and Seyff 58, Vadim Sadovski and Lena Miava 59, Rasulov 60r, Paper Street Design 61t, Shawna and Damien Richard 62l and 108t, Gumpanat and Triff 63, s_derevianko 64r, Antonio Guillem 65, sciencepics, Oleksandra Danilian, 5 second Studio, DenisNata, Eric Isselee, Dora Zett, Tuzemka and De Jongh Photography 66–67, Tsekhmister 68t, Tragoolchitr Jittasaiyapan 69, tobkatrina and shooarts 70, Allexxandar and Tuzemka 71, BUY THIS 74l, muratart and alex5711 75, Jagodka 79, 3DMAVR, KOKTARO and KatsiarynaKa2 80, Ekaterina Kolomeets 81, Eric Isselee and maximmmmum 82, FotoYakov 83b, Susan Schmitz 88b, Martin Capek, Grigorita Ko and photomaster 90, Linda Staf 93, Fesus Robert 94, Cre8tive Images and Mega Pixel 95, Sergey Moskvitin and Safar Aslanov 96, Elenarts 97, Yaska, Jumnong and Aphelleon 99, Kucher Serhii 102t, Artem Furman 103, e71lena 104–105, Vladi333 106t, FotoYakov 106b, Olist 107, Alex Coan 110t, Steve Heap 110b, Suzanne Tucker 111t, Nadzeya Harokh 111b; Wikimedia: Andrew Z. Colvin 76. 6l, N-studio 106r, DenisNata 108, nevodka 110, Tuzemka 111b.

Cats React cats from Shutterstock: Lubava, Seregraff, Jagodka and Getty: GlobalP, Arseniy45.

All design elements from Shutterstock.

Every attempt has been made to clear copyright. Should there be any inadvertent omission please apply to the publisher for rectification.

CONTENTS

Space is amazing! 4
What's out there? 6
Light years 10
The Big Bang 12
The Sun 14
Solar eclipse 18
Planets 20
Mercury 22
Venus 26
Earth 30
The Moon 34
Mars 36
The asteroid belt 40
Jupiter 42
Saturn 46
Uranus 50
Neptune 54
Dwarf planets 58
Meteoroids, meteors and meteorites 60
Comets 62

Stars 64
Nearby stars 68
Galaxies 70
The Milky Way 74
Groups and clusters 76
Dark matter and energy . . . 78
Weird space 80
Exoplanets 86
Black holes 90
The space race 92
Exploring space 96
Living in space 100
Searching for life 102
The future of space 104
Claw-ssary 108
Fur-ther information 111
Kitten-dex 112

SPACE IS AMAZING!

Did you know that the **FARAWAY** planet Kepler-16b **ORBITS TWO SUNS?**

Or that **STARS DON'T** actually **TWINKLE?** It's just **AN EFFECT** created by Earth's **ATMOSPHERE!**

I'm a rock star!

Discover **MIND-BLOWING SPACE FACTS** and **LAUGH** along with these **CRAZY CAT REACTIONS!** Do you **AGREE** with the **REACT-O-METER**?

Peace at last!

THERE'S ALMOST NO SOUND IN OUTER SPACE! THIS IS BECAUSE SPACE IS MADE UP OF LARGE EMPTY AREAS AND SOUND WAVES NEED TO BOUNCE OFF OBJECTS TO MAKE NOISE.

Wow! | No way! | OMG! | Gross! | Mind-blowing!

WHAT'S OUT THERE?

Our **PLANET, EARTH,** is part of a **SOLAR SYSTEM.**

In our solar system, **EARTH** and **SEVEN** other **PLANETS ORBIT** the **SUN**. Our solar system also contains many **SMALLER OBJECTS**, such as **ASTEROIDS, MOONS** and **DWARF PLANETS.**

The Sun

Earth

Mercury

Venus

The SUN is the LARGEST OBJECT in our SOLAR SYSTEM. Its GRAVITY pulls the PLANETS into ORBIT around it.

Uranus

Neptune

Jupiter

Saturn

Mars

In the PAST, some people thought that EARTH was at the CENTRE of our SOLAR SYSTEM and the OTHER PLANETS and the SUN ORBITED around it. It wasn't until the SIXTEENTH CENTURY that SCIENTISTS realised that the SUN was ACTUALLY at the CENTRE.

The universe stretches **FAR BEYOND** our solar system. It includes many more **STARS, PLANETS** and **GALAXIES.**

Caturn

Around **275 MILLION NEW STARS** are **BORN** in the universe **EVERY DAY.**

SOME SCIENTISTS SAY THAT THERE ARE **TEN TIMES** AS MANY **STARS** IN THE **UNIVERSE** AS THERE ARE **GRAINS OF SAND** ON EARTH!

Wow! | No way! | OMG! | Gross! | Mind-blowing!

LIGHT YEARS

The **UNIVERSE** is **SO HUGE** that we can't use kilometres to **MEASURE IT.** The numbers would be far too **HUGE!**

Instead, we use **LIGHT YEARS** to measure **DISTANCES** in the **UNIVERSE.** One light year is the **DISTANCE** that **LIGHT** travels in a **YEAR** (around **9 TRILLION KM**).

Good thing I'm so cat-letic!

THE UNIVERSE IS AROUND 93 BILLION LIGHT YEARS WIDE!

I've been floating fur-ever!

Wow! No way! OMG! Gross! Mind-blowing!

THE BIG BANG

Most **ASTRONOMERS** think that the **UNIVERSE** was **CREATED 13.8 BILLION YEARS AGO** after an **EXPLOSION** called the **BIG BANG**.

BEFORE the Big Bang, there was **NOTHING**. Then suddenly, the universe **EXPLODED** out of a **SINGLE POINT** (the Big Bang). Everything started **SPREADING OUT** and taking up more space.

At first, there were just tiny particles.

Particles came together to form atoms.

Over time, gravity pulled atoms together to make stars.

Groups of stars formed into galaxies.

The universe is still expanding today!

Our solar system formed about 4.5 billion years ago

THE STATIC BETWEEN CHANNELS ON OLD TVs WAS PARTLY MADE UP OF LEFTOVER ENERGY FROM THE BIG BANG!

Wow! No way! OMG! Gross! Mind-blowing!

THE SUN

The **SUN** is a **STAR!** It is a **MASSIVE BALL** of **HOT GAS.**

LIGHT and **HEAT** from the **SUN** travel to **EARTH** and the **OTHER PLANETS** in the **SOLAR SYSTEM.** Without **HEAT** from the **SUN**, Earth would be **TOO COLD** for **LIFE** as we know it.

It takes **EIGHT MINUTES** for **LIGHT ENERGY** to travel from the **SURFACE OF THE SUN** to **EARTH**. It takes **248 MINUTES** for **LIGHT ENERGY** to reach **NEPTUNE**.

I can get there in seven!

THE SUN IS **EXPANDING** ALL THE TIME. IN THE NEXT **5–7 BILLION YEARS**, THE **SUN** WILL **EXPAND** SO MUCH THAT IT WILL **ABSORB** AND **DESTROY EARTH!**

I'm getting out of here!

Wow! No way! OMG! Gross! Mind-blowing!

NUCLEAR REACTIONS take place in the **CORE (CENTRE)** of the **SUN**. This is what **PRODUCES** the **SUN'S ENERGY**.

The core is the hottest part of the Sun, with temperatures reaching up to 15 million °C!

Energy travels out from the core to the surface. The surface of the Sun is cooler – only 5,500 °C!

THE SURFACE OF THE SUN IS HOT ENOUGH TO BOIL DIAMONDS!

Purr-fectly hot!

No way! OMG! Gross!

Wow! Mind-blowing!

SOLAR ECLIPSE

Sometimes, the **SUN**, **MOON** and **EARTH LINE UP** to create a **TOTAL SOLAR ECLIPSE!**

Around once every **18 MONTHS**, the **MOON MOVES** between **EARTH** and the **SUN**. The Moon **COMPLETELY BLOCKS** the Sun and **CREATES A SHADOW ON SOME PARTS OF EARTH**. These places **GO DARK**. **ONLY THE ECLIPSE** can be **SEEN** in the sky, rather than **THE SUN**.

Zzzzzzzz

The only part of the Sun that can be seen during a total eclipse is the corona – the outer layer of the Sun's atmosphere.

COMPLETE DARKNESS can last up to **SEVEN AND A HALF MINUTES** during a **TOTAL SOLAR ECLIPSE.**

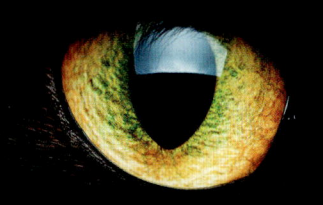

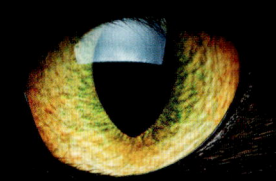

Good thing cats have great night vision!

PLANETS

What **EXACTLY** is a **PLANET**?

An **OBJECT** in **SPACE** has to have the following **FEATURES** to be considered a **PLANET**.

1 A planet has to be large enough for its gravity to make it into a roughly round shape.

2 A planet has to orbit a star.

Come here!

3 A planet has to have cleared its orbit of other objects by attracting them or repelling them.

THERE ARE MORE **PLANETS** THAN **STARS** IN OUR **GALAXY**, THE **MILKY WAY**.

A **GALAXY** is a **GROUP** of **STARS** (see pages 70–73).

Wow! No way! OMG! Gross! Mind-blowing!

MERCURY

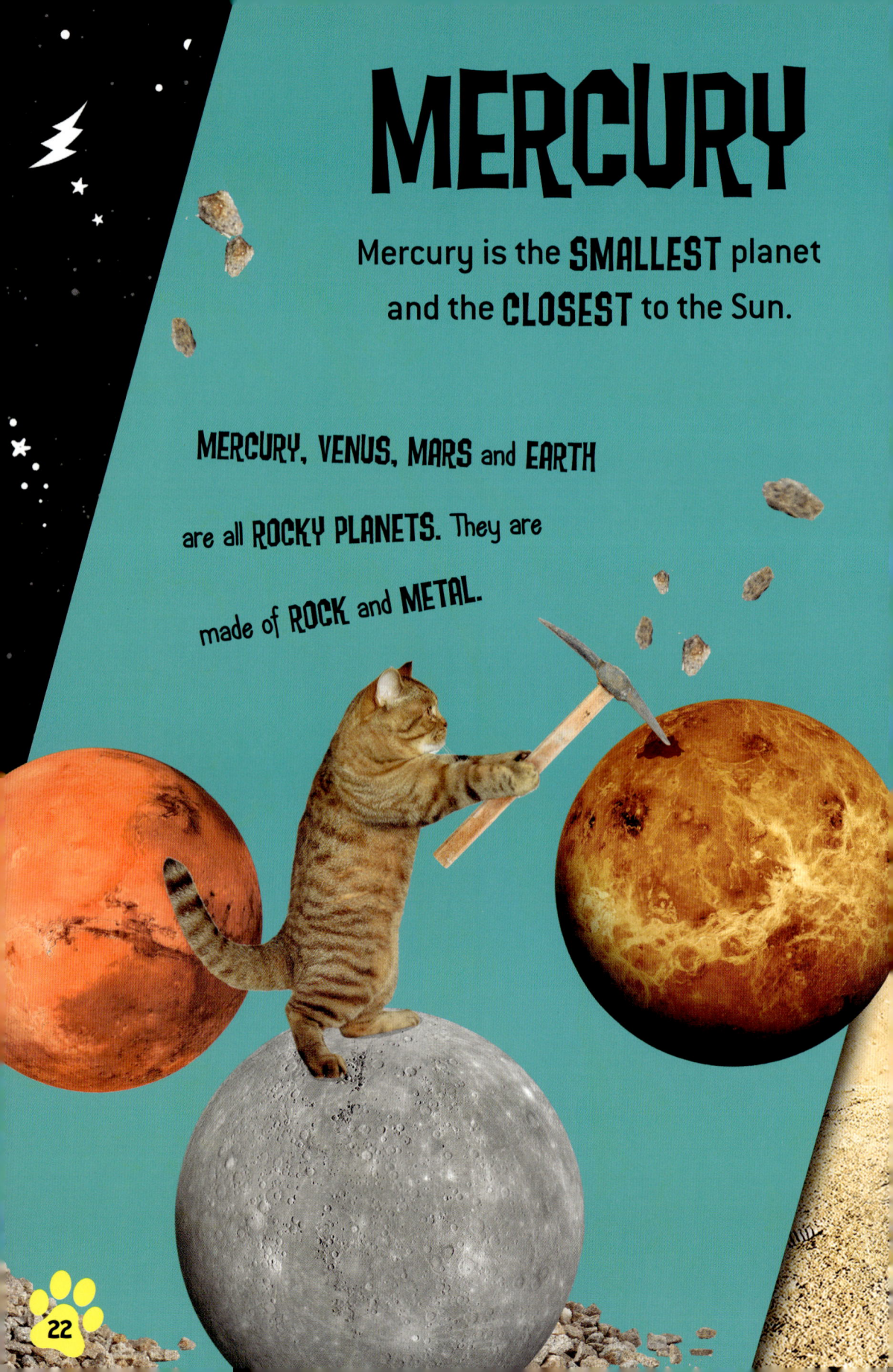

Mercury is the **SMALLEST** planet and the **CLOSEST** to the Sun.

MERCURY, VENUS, MARS and EARTH are all ROCKY PLANETS. They are made of ROCK and METAL.

Mercury is covered in **CRATERS** (holes in the ground). They were made when **COMETS** and **ASTEROIDS CRASHED** into its surface.

> Woah, this is deeper than I thought!

TEMPERATURES on Mercury are **VERY DIFFERENT** during the **DAY** and at **NIGHT**. This is because it doesn't have an **ATMOSPHERE** to **TRAP HEAT** from the Sun.

During the **DAY**, temperatures can reach **430°C**.

This heat is claw-ful!

At **NIGHT**, temperatures can drop to **-180°C**.

Brrrr, I'm fur-reezing!

IN SOME PLACES ON MERCURY, THE SUN **RISES**, **SETS** AND THEN **RISES** AGAIN EVERY MORNING! THIS IS BECAUSE MERCURY HAS AN EGG-SHAPED ORBIT.

My cat nap's confused!

VENUS

Venus is the **HOTTEST** planet in the solar system.

Venus is **SO HOT** because its **THICK ATMOSPHERE** traps **HEAT** from the Sun. It's so hot on Venus that it would **MELT LEAD!**

Meowsers!

Venus has **TENS** of **THOUSANDS** of **VOLCANOES.**

Another natural cat-astrophe!

Venus also has many mountains. Its **TALLEST MOUNTAIN,** Maxwell Montes, is around the **SAME HEIGHT** as **MOUNT EVEREST** (8,800 km), the **TALLEST MOUNTAIN** on Earth.

Venus is **CLOSER** to the Sun than Earth, so it only takes **225 DAYS** to **ORBIT** the Sun (**ONE VENUS YEAR**).

However, it **ROTATES** on its **AXIS** very slowly. It takes **243 DAYS** for Venus to rotate once (**ONE VENUS DAY**).

A DAY ON VENUS IS LONGER THAN A YEAR!

Days? Years? I'm furry confused!

Wow! | No way! | OMG! | Gross! | Mind-blowing!

EARTH

EARTH is **CONSTANTLY MOVING,** both in **ORBIT** around the **SUN** and on its **AXIS** (an imaginary line that runs through the North and South Pole).

> It takes **365¼ DAYS** for **EARTH** to **ORBIT** the **SUN.** This is **ONE EARTH YEAR.**

Earth is tilted as it orbits the Sun. This creates the seasons, as some parts of the planet are closer to the Sun than others.

It takes **24 HOURS** for **EARTH** to **SPIN ONCE** on its **AXIS**.
This is **ONE EARTH DAY.**

Day and night are created by Earth spinning on its axis. The side of the planet facing the Sun experiences day, while the other side experiences night.

EARTH'S STRUCTURE is made up of **DIFFERENT LAYERS**. The **OUTER SURFACE** of **EARTH** is called the **CRUST**. It is covered with **LAND** and **WATER**.

Holy furballs, that's hot!

Temperatures in the inner core can reach 5,400 °C! The inner core is the hottest part of Earth.

The outer core is made of liquid iron and nickel metals.

Earth's crust is approximately 70 km thick on land and 3-6 km thick under the oceans.

The mantle is a layer of very hot rock. Some of the rock in the mantle is so hot that it melts!

WATER COVERS OVER **70 PER CENT** OF EARTH'S SURFACE! **97 PER CENT** OF THIS WATER IS SALT WATER IN THE OCEAN.

Who says cats don't like water?

Wow! | No way! | OMG! | Gross! | Mind-blowing!

THE MOON

THE MOON orbits **EARTH**. It is **ONE** of **HUNDREDS OF MOONS** in our **SOLAR SYSTEM**.

The Moon appears to **CHANGE SHAPE** in the night sky. These shapes are called the **PHASES** of the **MOON**. This happens because **DIFFERENT PARTS** of the **MOON** are **LIT UP** by the **SUN** as the **MOON** turns on its **AXIS**.

It takes **29½ DAYS** for the **MOON** to go through all of its **PHASES** and return to its **ORIGINAL SHAPE**.

FIRST QUARTER

FULL MOON
(the full Moon can be seen in the sky)

NEW MOON
(no Moon can be seen in the sky)

LAST QUARTER

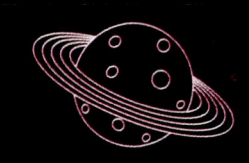

THE MOON IS FURTHER AWAY THAN IT LOOKS! 30 EARTH-SIZED PLANETS COULD FIT IN THE SPACE BETWEEN EARTH AND THE MOON!

Wow! | No way! | OMG! | Gross! | Mind-blowing!

MARS

Mars is known as the RED PLANET. It looks RED because of RUST in its ROCKS.

Humans have EXPLORED the surface of Mars with ROBOTIC ROVERS.

The rovers have found EVIDENCE of LIQUID WATER on Mars from BILLIONS OF YEARS AGO. TINY LIVING THINGS could have lived in these conditions, so there may have been LIFE ON MARS at one point!

Come look over here!

There is **STILL** some **WATER** on Mars today. However, it is mainly in the form of **ICE** at the **NORTH** and **SOUTH POLES** of the **PLANET**.

Ice is also found **DEEP** inside **CRATERS**, such as this one.

MARS has TWO MOONS - PHOBOS and DEIMOS. Both moons are POTATO-SHAPED! This is because they don't have ENOUGH GRAVITY to PULL THEIR MASS into a SPHERICAL SHAPE.

These cosmic chips are out of this world!

MARS IS HOME TO OLYMPUS MONS – THE TALLEST KNOWN VOLCANO IN THE UNIVERSE AT 22 KM HIGH.

22 km is a bit more than 235 Cat-tues of Liberty on top of each other!

Wow! | No way! | OMG! | Gross! | Mind-blowing!

39

THE ASTEROID BELT

Most of the **ASTEROIDS** in our **SOLAR SYSTEM** are found in a **BELT** between **MARS** and **JUPITER**.

ASTEROIDS are **SPACE ROCKS** that orbit the **SUN.** They were formed during the **CREATION** of our **SOLAR SYSTEM.**

Sometimes **ASTEROIDS CRASH** into each other and **BREAK DOWN** into smaller pieces. These smaller pieces can **FALL** to the **GROUND** on **EARTH** as **METEORITES.**

A **HUGE ASTEROID** CRASHING INTO **EARTH** PROBABLY LED TO THE **EXTINCTION** OF THE **DINOSAURS** 65 MILLION YEARS AGO!

Bye bye dinos!

Wow! | No way! | OMG! | Gross! | Mind-blowing!

JUPITER

Jupiter is the **LARGEST PLANET** in the solar system. It is **TWICE THE SIZE** of all the other planets combined.

Jupiter looks **SOLID**, but it's actually mainly made of **GAS**! It has a **SMALL SOLID CORE** under **THICK LAYERS OF GAS AND LIQUID**.

The **STRIPES** that we see on Jupiter are **CLOUDS** of **GAS** and **ICE FLOATING** in its **ATMOSPHERE**. Its **GIANT RED SPOT** is a **MASSIVE STORM**.

The storm has been going on for over one hundred years.

GIANT RED SPOT

Jupiter's Giant Red Spot is around twice the size of Earth.

43

Jupiter has **79 MOONS.**

Jupiter's largest moon, Ganymede, is larger than Mercury!

Europa is covered with a frozen icy crust, which may have liquid water underneath.

The moon Io has the most volcanoes of any object in the solar system.

The astronomer Galileo Galilei spotted Callisto, Io, Europa and Ganymede in 1610. They were the first objects in the solar system discovered using a telescope.

THE OCEAN UNDER THE SURFACE OF EUROPA IS THOUGHT TO CONTAIN TWICE THE AMOUNT OF WATER AS ALL THE OCEANS ON EARTH COMBINED.

Holy furballs!

Wow! · No way! · OMG! · Gross! · Mind-blowing!

SATURN

Saturn is WELL KNOWN for its BEAUTIFUL RINGS.

Saturn's rings are made up of BILLIONS OF PIECES of ROCK, ICE AND DUST. Some of the pieces are TINY SPECKS, while others are as LARGE AS HOUSES. A few are even as BIG AS MOUNTAINS!

Saturn is a **GAS GIANT**, like **JUPITER**.
It doesn't have a **SOLID SURFACE**,
but it probably has a **SOLID CORE**.

The rings orbit around Saturn.

Twice in every 29½ YEARS, Saturn's RINGS seem to DISAPPEAR! This is because of an OPTICAL ILLUSION. The POSITION of SATURN CHANGES so that we can only see the EDGES of its RINGS from Earth.

Are you kitten me? The rings were there a second ago!

48

SATURN'S RINGS ARE YOUNGER THAN THE DINOSAURS!

SATURN'S RINGS formed between **10** and **100 MILLION YEARS AGO**, while **DINOSAURS** first appeared **245 MILLION YEARS AGO**.

You rings are just kittens compared to me!

Wow! · No way! · OMG! · Gross! · Mind-blowing!

URANUS

Uranus is an **ICY** planet. It's **COLD** because it's so **FAR AWAY** from the Sun.

Uranus's **BLUE** colour comes from **METHANE GAS** in its **ATMOSPHERE**. It is surrounded by **13 RINGS** and **27 SMALL MOONS**.

This methane makes me feel sad and blue.

CLOUDS ON URANUS SMELL LIKE ROTTEN EGGS!

Wow! | No way! | OMG! | Gross! | Mind-blowing!

Unlike the other planets, Uranus **SPINS** on its **SIDE.**

Uranus's tilt gives it **VERY EXTREME SEASONS.** When it's **SUMMER** for Uranus's northern hemisphere, the south of the **PLANET** experiences a **TOTALLY DARK WINTER** that lasts **21 YEARS!**

See you in 21 years sunshine!

NEPTUNE

Neptune is the **FARTHEST PLANET** from the **SUN** in our **SOLAR SYSTEM**.

It is **COLD** and **DARK** on Neptune. This is because **LITTLE LIGHT** reaches the planet due to its **DISTANCE FROM THE SUN (4.5 BILLION KM)**.

Sunlight on Earth is 900 times brighter than the light that reaches Neptune.

I didn't need to pack my sunglasses after all!

Neptune is also the **WINDIEST PLANET** in the solar system, with winds of over **2,000 KPH.**

This wind makes me fur-ious!

WINDS on **NEPTUNE** can be **NINE TIMES STRONGER** than the most **POWERFUL STORMS** on **EARTH.**

55

NEPTUNE is named after the **ANCIENT ROMAN GOD** of the **SEA**. Its **13 MOONS** are named after **SEA GODS** and **MYTHICAL SEA CREATURES** from **ANCIENT GREEK LEGENDS**.

> I can't believe they didn't name one after the mythical miouw-maid!

ASTRONOMERS USED MATHS TO PREDICT THE EXISTENCE OF NEPTUNE BEFORE IT WAS ACTUALLY SEEN WITH A TELESCOPE!

I've got it!

What? Maybe I'm looking in the wrong place?

Wow! No way! OMG! Gross! Mind-blowing!

DWARF PLANETS

A dwarf planet is a **SMALL ROUND OBJECT** that **ORBITS** the **SUN.**

DWARF PLANETS are **MUCH SMALLER** than standard planets – smaller even than Earth's **MOON.** This means that they **DON'T HAVE** enough **GRAVITY** to **ATTRACT** or **REPEL** objects that lie in the **PATH OF THEIR ORBIT.**

CERES

ERIS

MAKEMAKE

There are five known dwarf planets.

HAUMEA

PLUTO

PLUTO HASN'T EVEN COMPLETED **ONE ORBIT** OF THE SUN SINCE IT WAS **DISCOVERED IN 1930!**

One Pluto year lasts 248 Earth years, so it won't finish its current orbit until the year 2178.

Over 150 years to go! Yawn!

Wow! | No way! | OMG! | Gross! | Mind-blowing!

METEOROIDS, METEORS AND METEORITES

METEOROIDS are **SMALL SPACE ROCKS** that sometimes get **CLOSE TO** and **LAND** on **OTHER PLANETS**.

A **METEOROID** could be as **SMALL** as a **GRAIN OF SAND**, or a **LARGE CHUNK** of **ROCK**.

Sometimes, meteoroids **ENTER THE ATMOSPHERE** of **EARTH** or another **PLANET**. They **BURN** and **EXPLODE** as they **FALL** through the **ATMOSPHERE**. These are known as **METEORS** or **SHOOTING STARS**.

Oh my paws! That's a fast one!

If a **METEOR** makes it through a **PLANET'S ATMOSPHERE** and **CRASHES** into the **GROUND**, it is called a **METEORITE**.

AROUND 44,000 KG OF METEORITES FALL TO EARTH EVERY DAY!

You can never be too careful!

Wow! · No way! · OMG! · Gross! · Mind-blowing!

COMETS

A **COMET** is an **ICY BALL** of **FROZEN GAS** and **ROCK** that **ORBITS** the **SUN**.

Most **COMETS** come from the **COLD EDGES** of the **SOLAR SYSTEM**, beyond **NEPTUNE**. When they get **CLOSE** to the **SUN**, the comet's **ICE HEATS UP** and **MELTS**. This creates a **GIANT GLOWING CLOUD**.

Gas and **DUST** are **RELEASED** from the comet and form **LONG TAILS**.

You call that a tail?

HALLEY'S COMET CAN BE SEEN FROM EARTH ON AVERAGE EVERY 76 YEARS. IT WILL NEXT APPEAR IN 2061.

Wake me up in 2061!

No way! OMG! Gross!

Wow! Mind-blowing!

STARS

Stars are **GIANT BALLS** of **HOT GAS**.

Stars are mainly made up of **HYDROGEN** and **HELIUM GASES**. **INSIDE A STAR, HYDROGEN** is turned into **HELIUM**. This creates a **HUGE** amount of **ENERGY**, which makes **STARS GLOW**.

Twinkle, twinkle little star

THE STAR KEPLER 11145123 IS THE MOST PERFECTLY ROUND NATURAL OBJECT EVER OBSERVED!

Wow! · **No way!** · **OMG!** · **Gross!** · **Mind-blowing!**

65

Stars are **DIFFERENT SIZES** and **COLOURS** at different points in their **LIFE CYCLE**.

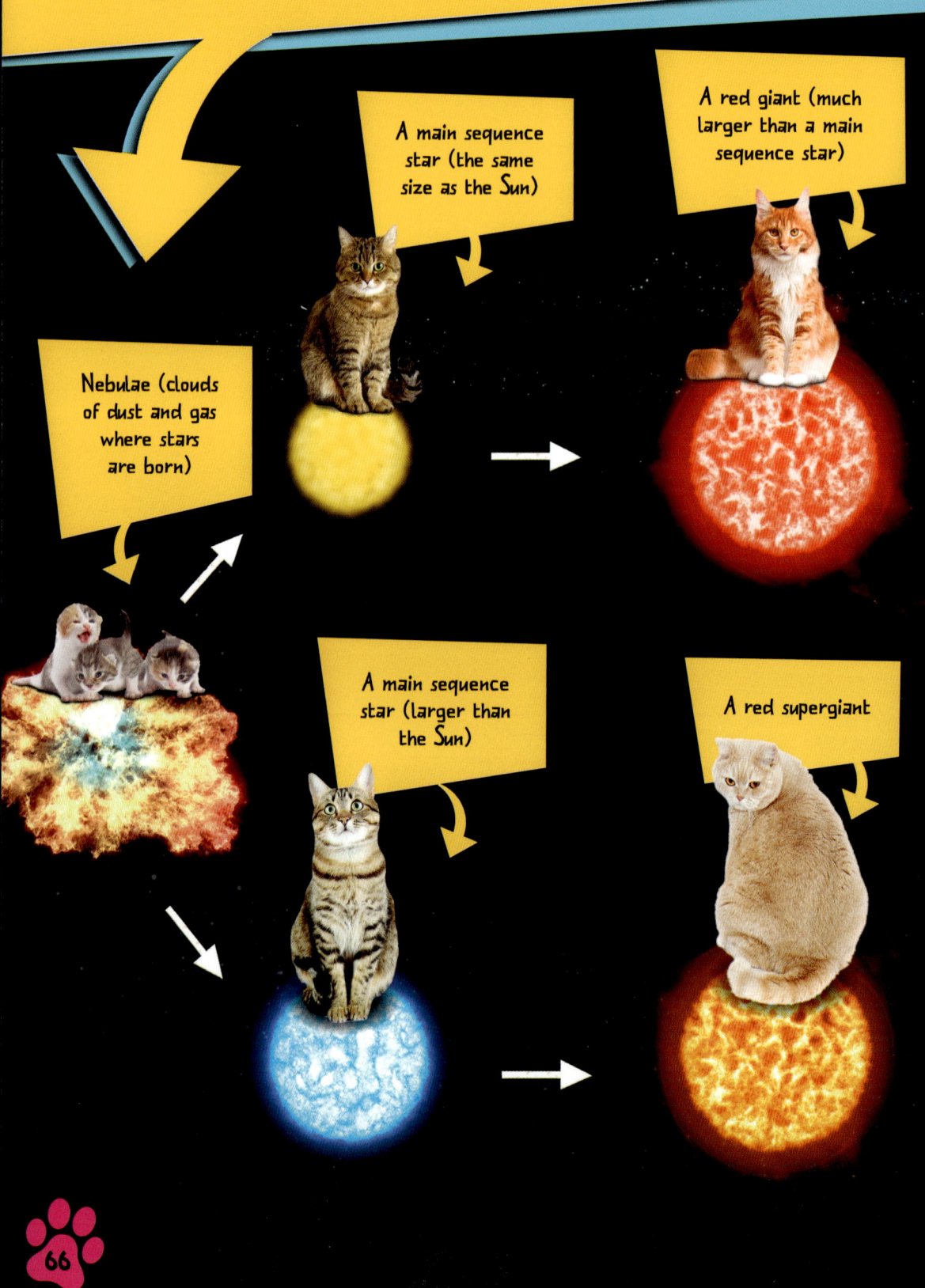

Nebulae (clouds of dust and gas where stars are born)

A main sequence star (the same size as the Sun)

A red giant (much larger than a main sequence star)

A main sequence star (larger than the Sun)

A red supergiant

A planetary nebula (a shell of hot gas)

A white dwarf (the cool remains of a star)

A neutron star (the dense remains of a star's core)

A supernova (huge explosion)

A black hole (see pages 90-91)

NEARBY STARS

The stars in **ALPHA CENTAURI** are some of the **NEAREST STARS** to **EARTH,** at just **OVER FOUR LIGHT YEARS AWAY!**

ALPHA CENTAURI is a **SYSTEM** made up of **THREE STARS. TWIN STARS ALPHA CENTAURI A** and **B ORBIT** around a **CENTRAL POINT OF GRAVITY.** This is known as a **BINARY STAR.**

Twins, just like us!

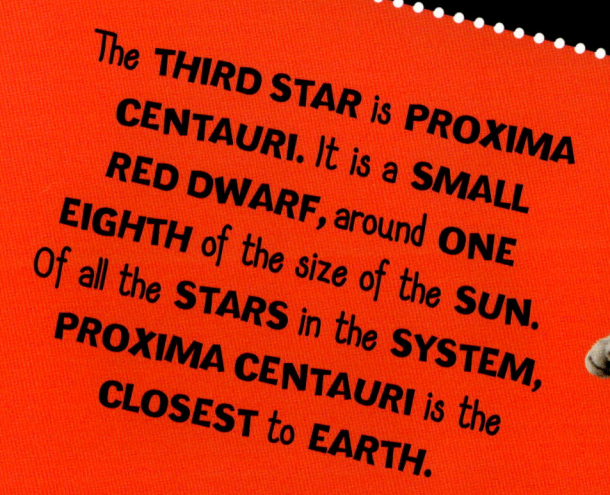

The **THIRD STAR** is **PROXIMA CENTAURI**. It is a **SMALL RED DWARF**, around **ONE EIGHTH** of the size of the **SUN**. Of all the **STARS** in the **SYSTEM**, **PROXIMA CENTAURI** is the **CLOSEST** to **EARTH**.

There it is!

ALPHA CENTAURI A AND B ARE SEEN FROM EARTH AS A SINGLE STAR. TOGETHER, THEY ARE THE **FOURTH BRIGHTEST STAR** IN THE **NIGHT SKY!**

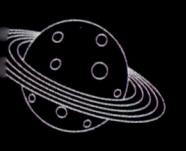

GALAXIES

A **GALAXY** is a **GROUP** of **MILLIONS OF STARS** held together by **GRAVITY**.

There are **THREE MAIN SHAPES** of **GALAXY** – **SPIRAL, ELLIPTICAL** and **IRREGULAR**. More than **TWO THIRDS** of galaxies are **SPIRAL GALAXIES**.

spiral – spiral arms around a central bulge

spiral

elliptical

irregular

elliptical – round or oval shape

irregular – no distinguishable shape

A SPIRAL GALAXY

Most of the stars in a spiral galaxy are found in the centre. The dark streaks in the arms of the galaxy are made up of dust. The stars in the galaxy's arms are mostly young stars. This is why they shine so brightly.

Galaxies can **INTERACT** with each other if they get **TOO CLOSE. LARGER GALAXIES** often **STEAL STARS** from **SMALLER GALAXIES.** The larger galaxy's **GRAVITY** pulls stars away.

Cat burglar ... me?

If **TWO GALAXIES CRASH** into each other, they can **MERGE** to **FORM** a **NEW GALAXY.**

THE **HUBBLE SPACE TELESCOPE** ONCE FOUND **10,000 GALAXIES** IN **ONE IMAGE** OF **SPACE!**

That's fur too many to count!

No way! OMG! Gross! Wow! Mind-blowing!

73

THE MILKY WAY

Our **SOLAR SYSTEM** is in a **GALAXY** called the **MILKY WAY**.

The **MILKY WAY** is a **SPIRAL GALAXY**. It contains **HUNDREDS OF BILLIONS** of **STARS**, including **OUR STAR**, the **SUN**.

Our solar system is on a spur (short arm) of the Milky Way. It's about 25,000 light years from the centre of the galaxy.

A SPUR

Did someone say milk?

OUR SOLAR SYSTEM

SCIENTISTS PREDICT THAT THE **MILKY WAY** WILL **CRASH INTO** ITS **NEAREST NEIGHBOURING GALAXY**, THE **ANDROMEDA GALAXY**, IN **4.5 BILLION YEARS!**

Did someone say crash? I'm out of here!

Wow! | No way! | OMG! | Gross! | Mind-blowing!

GROUPS AND CLUSTERS

Galaxies are often found together in **GROUPS** or **CLUSTERS**.

There are usually no more than **FIFTY GALAXIES** in a **GALAXY GROUP**. Larger **GROUPS** of **GALAXIES** are known as **CLUSTERS**. **SUPERCLUSTERS** are made up of many **SMALLER CLUSTERS** or **GROUPS**.

The Milky Way is part of a group called the Local Group.

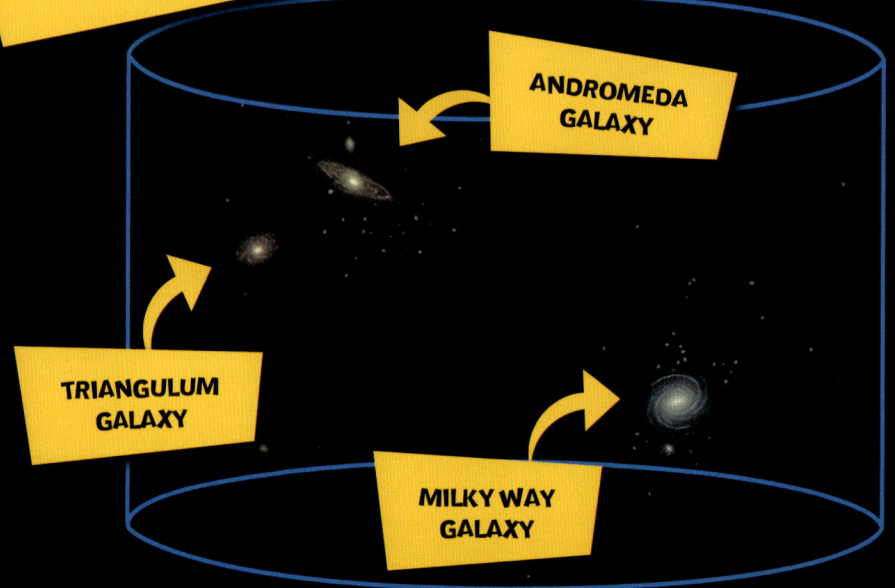

ANDROMEDA GALAXY

TRIANGULUM GALAXY

MILKY WAY GALAXY

SUPERCLUSTERS ARE THE LARGEST STRUCTURES IN THE UNIVERSE!

We're a super-claw-ster!

Wow! · No way! · OMG! · Gross! · Mind-blowing!

DARK MATTER AND ENERGY

EVERYTHING that we can SEE in SPACE is a VERY SMALL PART of the UNIVERSE. The rest is MYSTERIOUS DARK MATTER and DARK ENERGY.

We use the word MATTER to describe EVERYTHING VISIBLE that EXISTS in the UNIVERSE, from EARTH to STARS and GALAXIES. However, scientists have also noticed an INVISIBLE TYPE OF MATTER that has a GRAVITATIONAL EFFECT on objects in SPACE. They can't see this DARK MATTER, but they know it's there.

I'll get you! I can't see you, but I know you're there!

Around TWO THIRDS of the UNIVERSE is made up of INVISIBLE DARK ENERGY. Like DARK MATTER, scientists can't see DARK ENERGY, but they know that it is making the UNIVERSE EXPAND.

TOGETHER, DARK MATTER AND DARK ENERGY MAKE UP 95 PER CENT OF THE UNIVERSE!

How much of the universe is black cat-ter?!

Wow! No way! OMG! Gross! Mind-blowing!

WEIRD SPACE

SPACE is full of **WEIRD** and **WONDERFUL** things!

Humans **HAVEN'T TRAVELLED FAR** in space, but we have been able to learn about **STRANGE** and **INCREDIBLE THINGS** beyond our solar system, thanks to **TELESCOPES** and **SPACECRAFT** (see pages 96–99).

HYPERVELOCITY STARS zoom through the universe at **SPEEDS** of over **2 MILLION KPH!** They reach these speeds because they are **THROWN OUT OF GALAXIES**, as if they were in a **SLINGSHOT**.

The **SAGITTARIUS B2 DUST CLOUD** smells like **RUM** and tastes like **RASPBERRIES!** This is because it contains **CHEMICALS** that give these foods their **TASTE** and **SMELL**.

A **GIANT JET** of **MATTER** is shooting out of **GALAXY 3C303**. The jet carries **THE HIGHEST ELECTRICAL CURRENT** ever observed, equivalent to **ONE TRILLION BOLTS OF LIGHTNING!**

Two huge **MYSTERIOUS BUBBLES** made up of **GAMMA RAYS** and **GAS** are found **ABOVE** and **BELOW** the **MILKY WAY**. Scientists think that they may be formed by the **BLACK HOLE** at the **CENTRE** of the galaxy (see pages 90–91).

GAMMA RAY BUBBLE

MILKY WAY

In 2017, our solar system welcomed its **FIRST KNOWN VISITOR** from another **STAR SYSTEM** – the **MYSTERIOUS LOG-SHAPED 'OUMUAMUA!** It measured around **400 M LONG** and **UP TO 4000 M WIDE, UNLIKE ANYTHING SEEN** in our solar system **BEFORE.**

We're on an interstellar miouw-ssion!

At first, there were **WORRIES** it could be an **ALIEN SPACECRAFT!** But **SCIENTISTS** confirmed that 'Oumuamua is **JUST A ROCK.** They believe it had been **MOVING** through the **MILKY WAY** for **MILLIONS OF YEARS** before passing through **OUR SOLAR SYSTEM.**

HOAG'S OBJECT is a very **CURIOUS GALAXY**. **NOTHING APPEARS TO CONNECT** the **YELLOW CENTRE** of the galaxy, made up of **OLD STARS**, to its **BLUE OUTER RING**, made up of **NEW STARS!** It's as if someone has **CLEANED** the **CONNECTING STARS AWAY**.

Purr-haps I need to get the hoover out ...

However, scientists believe that the two parts of the galaxy may be connected by stars that are too faint to see.

EXOPLANETS

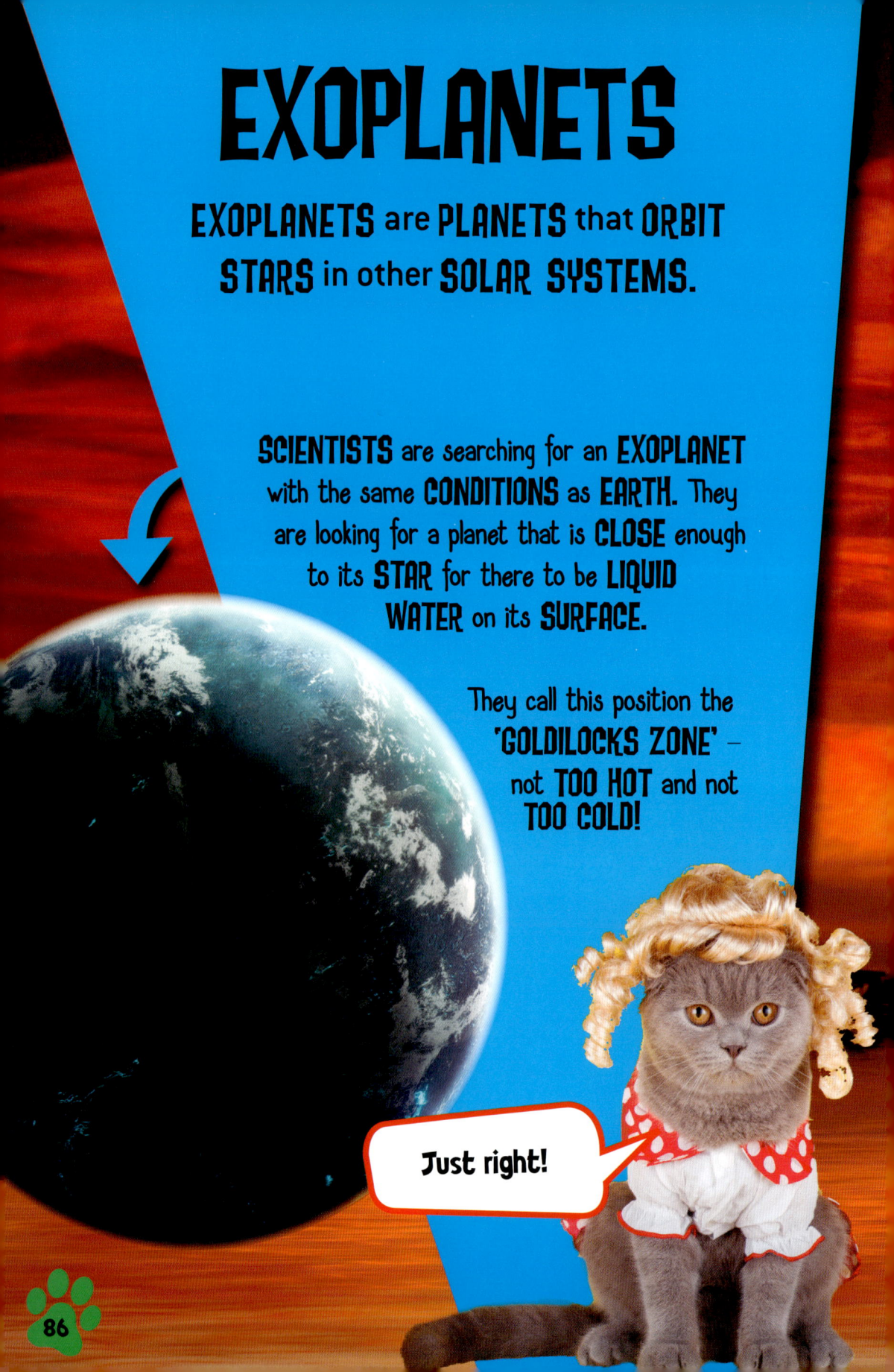

EXOPLANETS are **PLANETS** that **ORBIT STARS** in other **SOLAR SYSTEMS**.

SCIENTISTS are searching for an **EXOPLANET** with the same **CONDITIONS** as **EARTH**. They are looking for a planet that is **CLOSE** enough to its **STAR** for there to be **LIQUID WATER** on its **SURFACE**.

They call this position the **'GOLDILOCKS ZONE'** – not **TOO HOT** and not **TOO COLD!**

Just right!

One day, **HUMANS** may be able to live on an **EXOPLANET** in the **GOLDILOCKS ZONE!**

Some EXOPLANETS are VERY STRANGE ...

It could **RAIN GLASS** on exoplanet Hd 189733b! This is because its atmosphere contains **SILICATES**, which turn into glass when **HEATED UP**.

The exoplanet 55 Cancri e could contain a **HUGE AMOUNT OF DIAMONDS!** This is because it contains large amounts of **CARBON**, which will probably turn into diamond under the **HIGH HEAT** and **PRESSURE** found on this planet!

One ticket to 55 Cancri e please!

Fur-prise!

Exoplanet Wasp 12 b is being **STRETCHED INTO AN EGG SHAPE** by the gravity of the star in its solar system.

89

BLACK HOLES

A **BLACK HOLE** is a **SINGLE SMALL POINT** that is packed full of **MATTER.**

A black hole's **GRAVITY** is **SO STRONG** that almost **NOTHING CAN ESCAPE IT**, not even light! Black holes are formed when **MASSIVE STARS COLLAPSE** and **EXPLODE** at the end of their life cycle.

There are **HUGE BLACK HOLES** at the **CENTRE** of most **GALAXIES**, including the **MILKY WAY.**

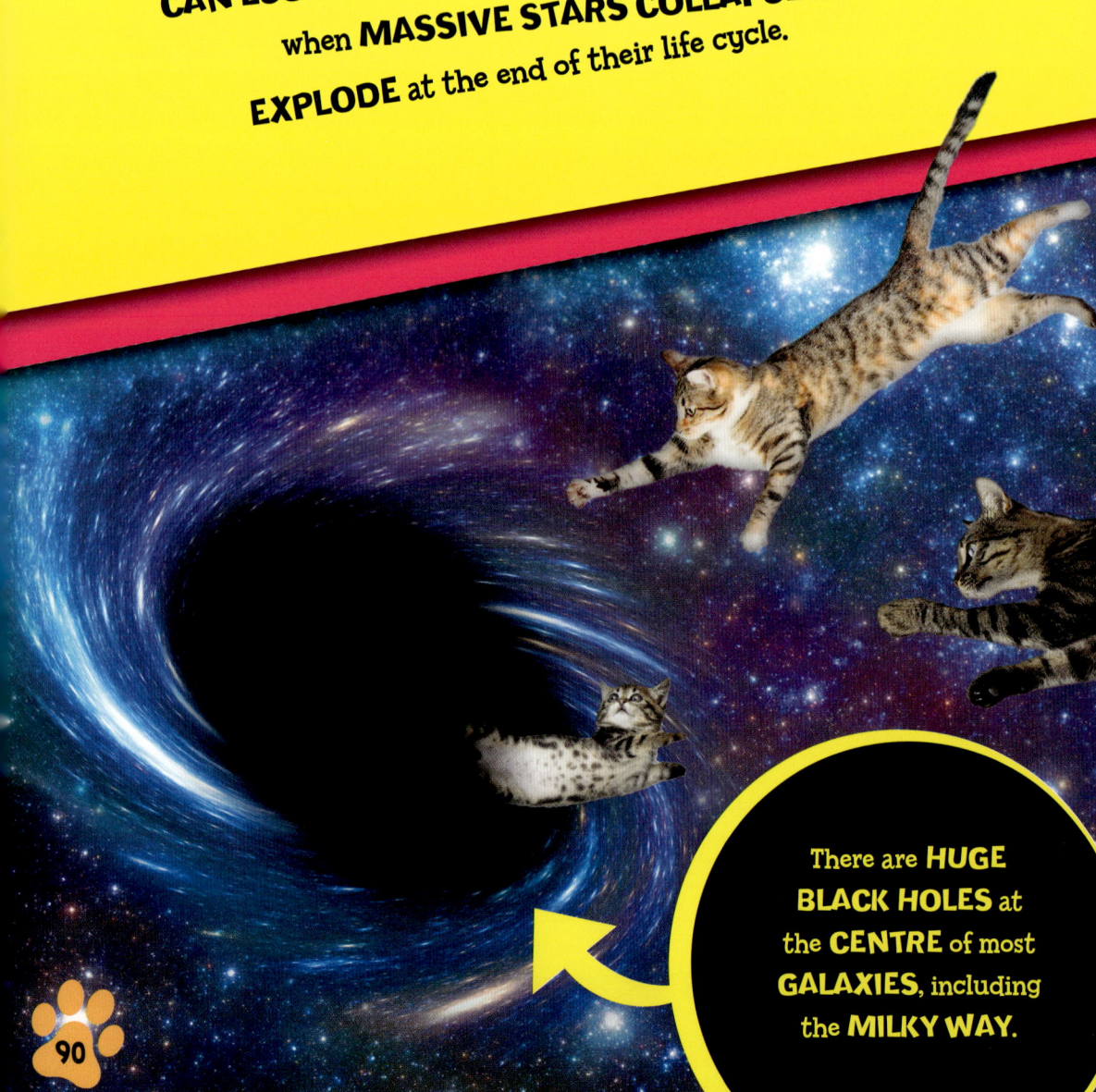

ANYTHING THAT **FELL** INTO A **BLACK HOLE** WOULD BE **STRETCHED OUT** LIKE A LONG PIECE OF **SPAGHETTI!** SCIENTISTS CALL THIS PROCESS **'SPAGHETTIFICATION!'**

Oh no! I've been spaghetti-fied!

Wow! · No way! · OMG! · Gross! · Mind-blowing!

THE SPACE RACE

The **RACE** to **EXPLORE SPACE** started in the **1950s**.

During the **SPACE RACE**, the **USA** and the **SOVIET UNION** (a group of countries including Russia) **COMPETED** with each other to be the **FIRST** to **EXPLORE SPACE**.

In 1957, the **SOVIET UNION** took an early lead when they sent the **SATELLITE SPUTNIK 1** into **SPACE**. It was the **FIRST OBJECT** to **ORBIT EARTH**.

The **FIRST ANIMAL** to **ORBIT EARTH** was the **DOG LAIKA.** She travelled into space in a **SOVIET SATELLITE** in **1957.**

What about the first cat-stronaut?!

The USA made a HUGE LEAP in SPACE EXPLORATION when the APOLLO 11 ASTRONAUTS landed on the MOON in 1969. This was the FIRST TIME that HUMANS had EXPLORED another body in space. To this day, the Moon remains the ONLY OTHER BODY IN SPACE VISITED by HUMANS.

Did you bring me food in your spaceship?

A **FELT-TIP PEN** SAVED THE **LIVES** OF THE **APOLLO 11 ASTRONAUTS!** THEY USED THE **PEN** TO **FIX A BROKEN SWITCH** THAT WOULD HAVE MEANT THAT THEY **COULDN'T TAKE OFF** FROM THE **MOON.**

Wow! | No way! | OMG! | Gross! | Mind-blowing!

EXPLORING SPACE

Since the space race, many **SPACECRAFT** have been sent into space for **RESEARCH**.

SPACECRAFT have **ORBITED** and **LANDED** on planets and other bodies in space, such as asteroids. They **SEND BACK INFORMATION** to Earth.

Holy furballs! We've been rumbled!

SPACECRAFT OFTEN USE PLANETS' GRAVITY AS A SLINGSHOT TO SHOOT THEM QUICKLY THROUGH SPACE, RATHER THAN USING PRECIOUS FUEL.

Wheee!

Wow! No way! OMG! Gross! Mind-blowing!

97

SPACE TELESCOPES take photos of **DEEP SPACE, BILLIONS OF LIGHT YEARS** away from our solar system. They have sent back **PHOTOS** of **STARS BEING BORN, DISTANT GALAXIES** and **STRANGE EXOPLANETS** (see pages 86–89).

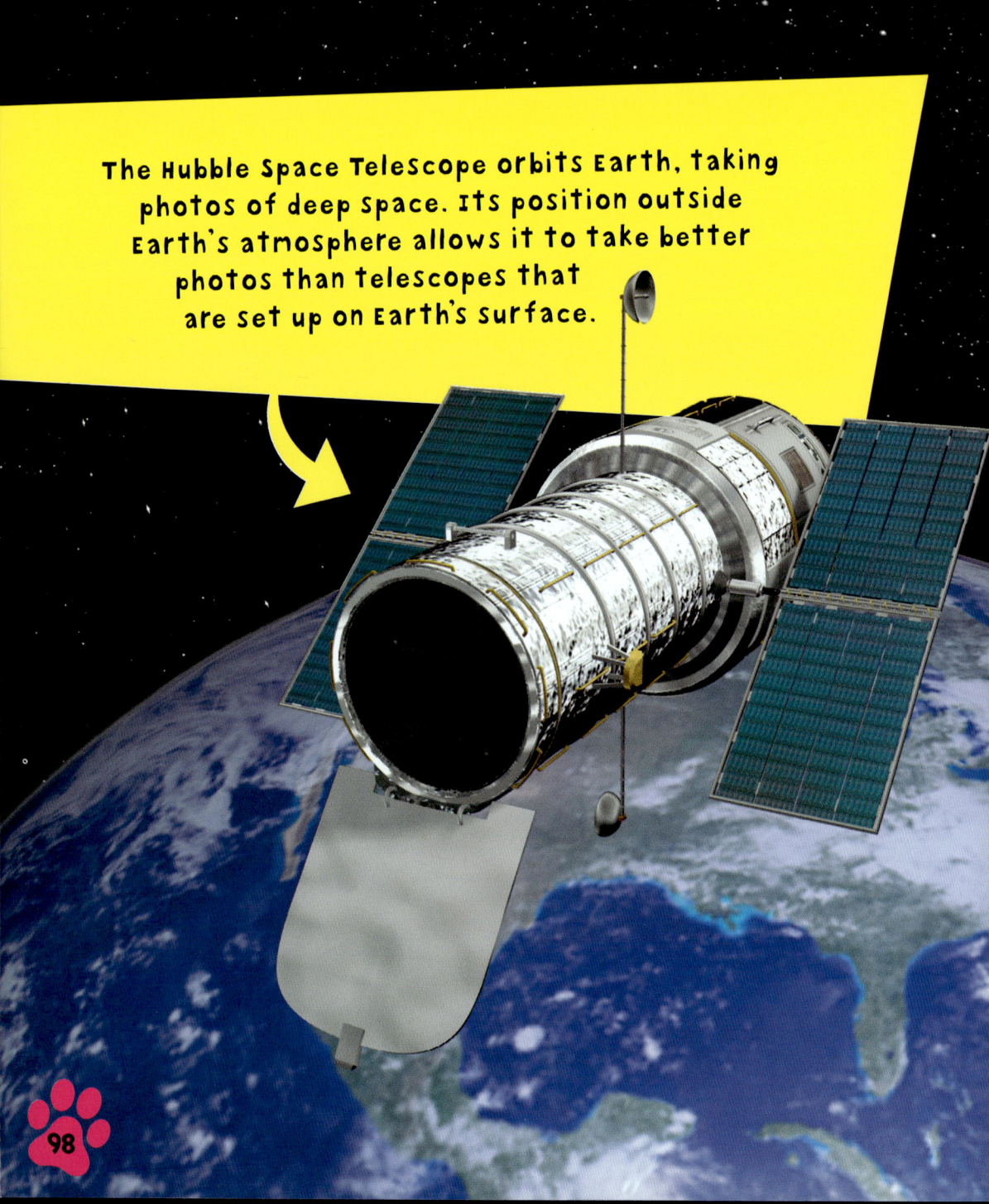

The Hubble Space Telescope orbits Earth, taking photos of deep space. Its position outside Earth's atmosphere allows it to take better photos than telescopes that are set up on Earth's surface.

PHOTOS FROM DEEP SPACE

A GALAXY

A BRIGHT DISTANT STAR

A NEBULA, WHERE STARS ARE BORN

LIVING IN SPACE

Some people **LIVE** in **SPACE** for **WEEKS** or even **MONTHS!**

ASTRONAUTS from all over the world **LIVE IN SPACE** on the **INTERNATIONAL SPACE STATION** (ISS). The ISS is a **SATELLITE** that **ORBITS** Earth. Astronauts do **EXPERIMENTS** on the ISS to learn more about how being in **SPACE AFFECTS HUMANS.**

I'm the first cat-stronaut!

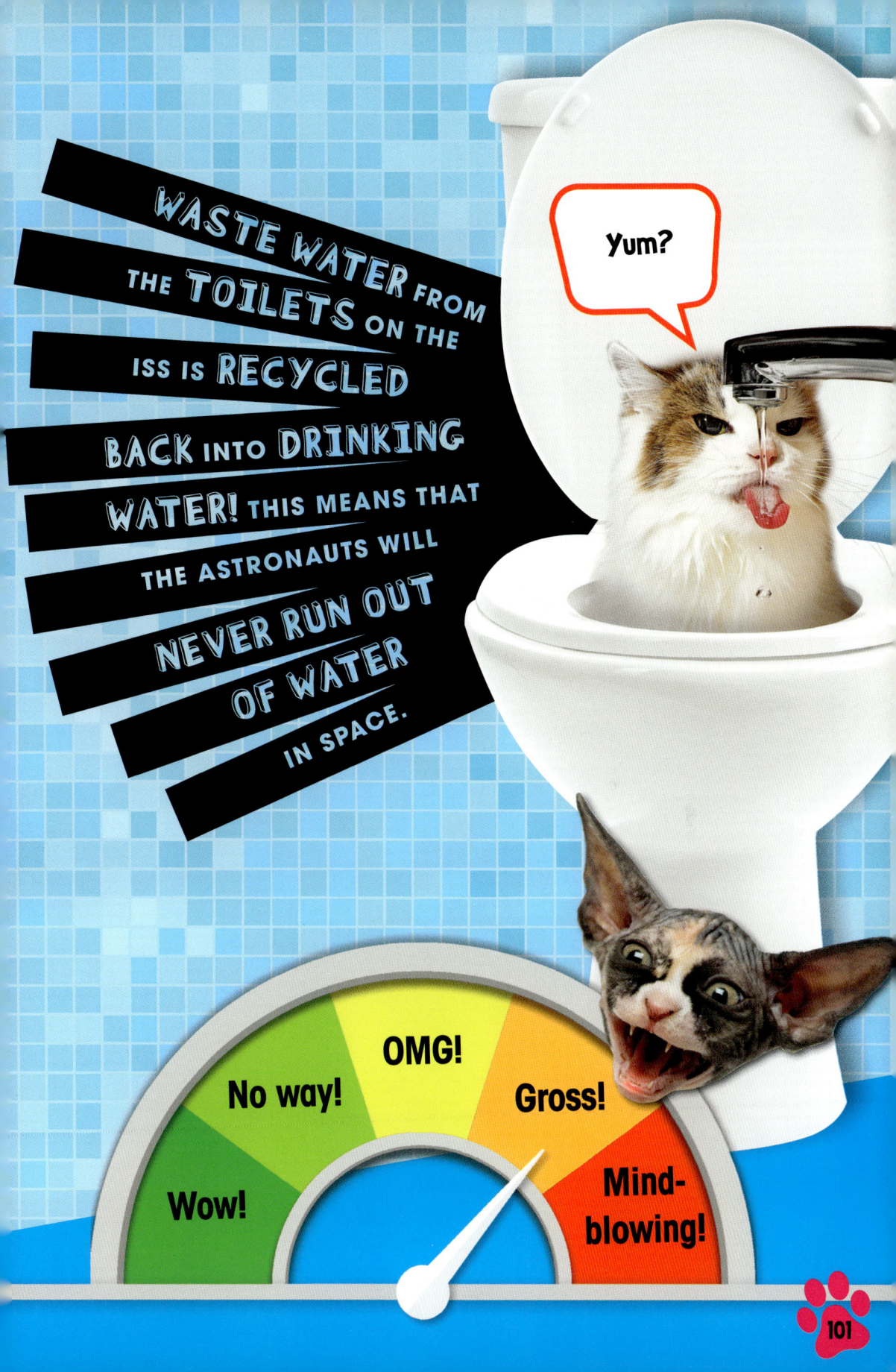

WASTE WATER FROM THE TOILETS ON THE ISS IS RECYCLED BACK INTO DRINKING WATER! THIS MEANS THAT THE ASTRONAUTS WILL NEVER RUN OUT OF WATER IN SPACE.

Yum?

Wow! | No way! | OMG! | Gross! | Mind-blowing!

SEARCHING FOR LIFE

Many people WONDER if we are ALONE in the UNIVERSE, or if ALIEN LIFE is OUT THERE!

It's quite UNLIKELY that Earth is the ONLY PLANET in the UNIVERSE that CONTAINS LIFE. Scientists MONITOR RADIO WAVES from SPACE to see if they can pick up ALIEN SIGNALS. So far, they haven't found anything.

Can you repeat that?

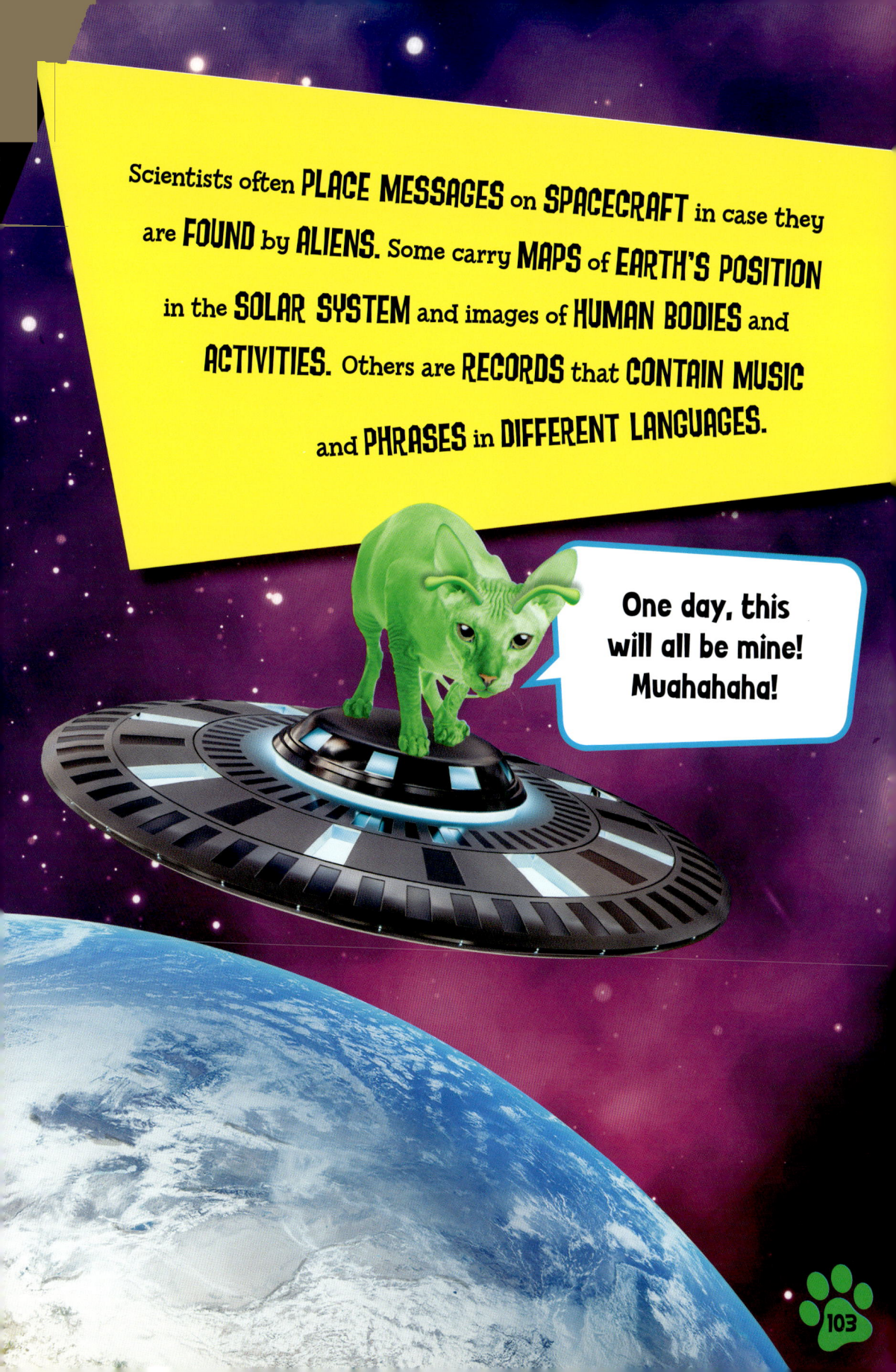

Scientists often **PLACE MESSAGES** on **SPACECRAFT** in case they are **FOUND** by **ALIENS**. Some carry **MAPS** of **EARTH'S POSITION** in the **SOLAR SYSTEM** and images of **HUMAN BODIES** and **ACTIVITIES**. Others are **RECORDS** that **CONTAIN MUSIC** and **PHRASES** in **DIFFERENT LANGUAGES**.

One day, this will all be mine! Muahahaha!

THE FUTURE OF SPACE

SCIENTISTS are currently planning **EXCITING** and **GROUNDBREAKING TRIPS** to **SPACE**.

NASA is **PLANNING** to send **HUMANS TO MARS** at some point in the future. However, they need to do **MORE RESEARCH** first. They have **PLANNED MORE ROVER MISSIONS** to the planet to **LEARN MORE** about it.

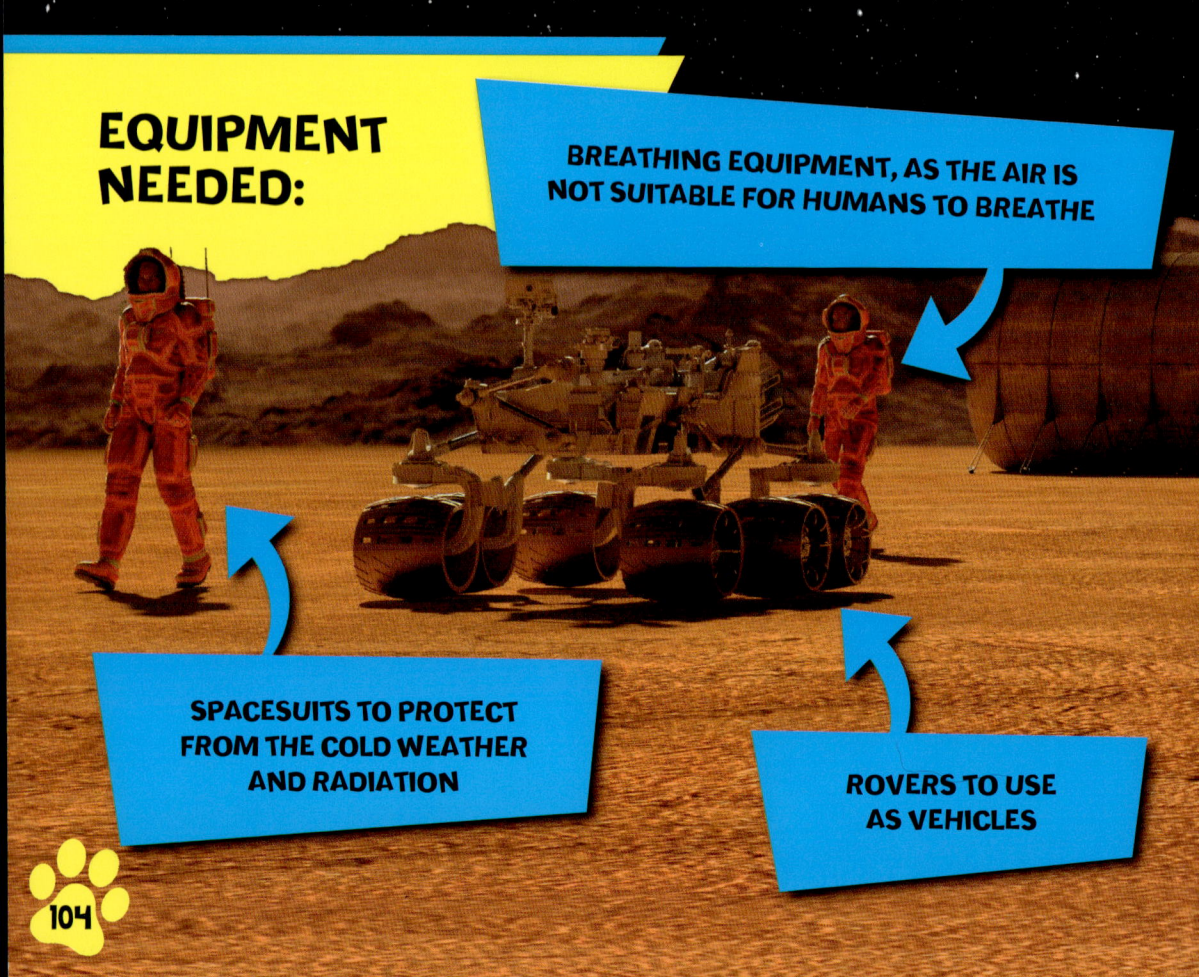

EQUIPMENT NEEDED:

- BREATHING EQUIPMENT, AS THE AIR IS NOT SUITABLE FOR HUMANS TO BREATHE
- SPACESUITS TO PROTECT FROM THE COLD WEATHER AND RADIATION
- ROVERS TO USE AS VEHICLES

SCIENTISTS believe that it might be **POSSIBLE** for **HUMANS** to **LIVE ON MARS**, as the **CONDITIONS** are **SIMILAR** to those on **EARTH**. However, a **COLONY** on **MARS** would be very **DIFFERENT** to **LIFE ON EARTH**.

HABITATS TO SHELTER AND DO RESEARCH

GREENHOUSES TO GROW FOOD

I've always wanted to live on Miaouws!

So far, **NEARLY EVERYONE** who has travelled into space has been an **ASTRONAUT**. However, some **COMPANIES** are currently looking into **SPACE TOURISM.** They hope that one day, **ORDINARY PEOPLE** will be able to travel into **SPACE** for a **HOLIDAY!**

What have I fur-gotten?!

THE **FIRST SPACE TOURIST** FLEW TO THE **ISS** IN **2001.** THE TRIP COST **US$20 MILLION!**

WOULD YOU LIKE TO TRAVEL INTO SPACE?

No way!
OMG!
Gross!
Wow!
Mind-blowing!

107

CLAW-SSARY

asteroid - a space rock that orbits the Sun

astronomer - someone who studies the universe

atmosphere - the gases that surround Earth and other planets

atom - the smallest possible amount of a substance

axis - an imaginary line that goes through the centre of an object

binary star - two stars that orbit around a central point

black hole - a single point with such strong gravity that almost nothing can escape its pull

cluster - a large group of more than fifty galaxies

colony - a group of people who live together in an area that is far away from others

comet - a frozen ball of gas and rock that orbits the Sun

core - the central part of something

corona - the outer atmosphere of the Sun

crater - a large hole in the ground

crust - the outer layer of a planet's structure

dark energy - an invisible type of energy that makes up around two thirds of the universe

dark matter - an invisible type of matter that has a gravitational effect on objects in space

dwarf planet - a round object that orbits the Sun, which is smaller than a planet but doesn't have enough gravity to clear its orbit path of smaller objects

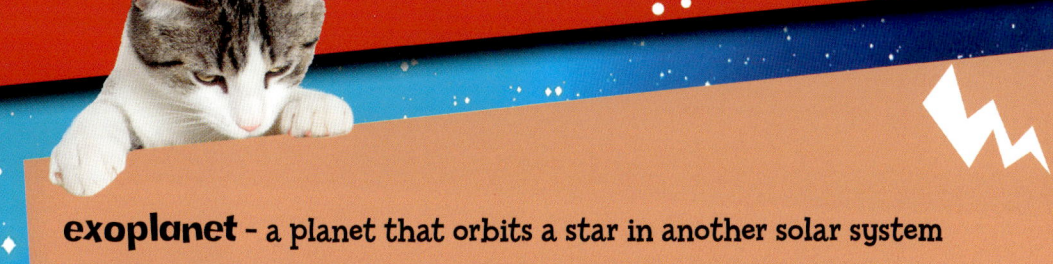

exoplanet - a planet that orbits a star in another solar system

extinction - when all of a species dies out and the species no longer exists

galaxy - a group of stars

gas - a substance that has a form like air and can move freely around

gravity - a force that pulls things towards each other

group - a group of no more than fifty galaxies

hemisphere - one half of a planet

light year - the distance that light travels in a year (roughly 9 trillion km)

liquid - a substance that can flow and take the shape of a container

main sequence star - a stable star that is turning hydrogen gas into helium gas

mantle - the middle layer of a planet's structure

melt - to turn from a solid into a liquid

meteor - a meteoroid that has entered the atmosphere of a planet

meteorite - a small space rock that falls to the surface of a planet or a moon

meteoroid - a small space rock

nebula - a cloud of dust and gas where stars are created

neutron star - the dense remains of a star's core

orbit - to travel around a planet or a star in a curved path

particle - a very small piece of something

planetary nebula - a shell of hot gass

pressure - a force that presses on things

red giant - a dying star

red supergiant - a large dying star

repel - to force something to move away

rover - a small vehicle that can move over rough ground

satellite - an object that orbits a larger object in space

solar eclipse - when the Sun disappears from view on Earth because the Moon blocks its path

solid - a substance with a fixed shape that always take up the same amount of space

spherical - describes something that has a sphere shape, like a 3D circle

spur - a small arm that comes off of a galaxy

supercluster - a very large group of smaller galaxy clusters

supernova - a star that has exploded

white dwarf - the cool remains of a star

FUR-THER INFORMATION

BOOKS
A Guide to Space
by Kevin Pettman (Wayland, 2020)

Earth and Space (Science in a Flash)
by Georgia Amson-Bradshaw (Franklin Watts, 2018)

Infomojis: Space
by Jon Richards and Ed Simkins (Wayland, 2018)

WEBSITES
www.factslides.com/s-Solar-System
Astonish your friends with these facts about the solar system.

www.jpl.nasa.gov/edu/pdfs/ss-extreme-poster.pdf
Print out a poster of some of the most extreme space facts.

www.natgeokids.com/uk/discover/science/space/ten-facts-about-space
Discover 10 more amazing facts about space.

KITTEN-DEX

alien life 84, 102-103
Alpha Centauri 68-69
Apollo 11 94, 95
asteroid belt, the 40-41
asteroids 6, 23, 40, 41, 96
atmospheres 4, 18, 24, 26, 43, 50, 60, 61, 88, 98

Big Bang, the 12-13
black holes 67, 83, 90-91

clusters 76
comets 23, 62-63

dark energy 78, 79
dark matter 78, 79
dwarf planets 6, 58-59

Earth 4, 6, 7, 14, 15, 18, 22, 30-33, 34, 35, 40, 41, 43, 48, 55, 60, 61, 63, 68, 69, 78, 86, 92, 93, 96, 98, 100, 102, 103, 105
exoplanets 86-89, 98

galaxies 8, 12, 21, 70-73, 74, 75, 76, 78, 80, 82, 83, 85, 90, 98, 99
gamma ray bubbles 83
gravity 7, 12, 20, 38, 58, 68, 70, 72, 78, 89, 90, 97
groups 76

Hubble Space Telescope 73, 98
hypervelocity stars 80

International Space Station, the 100, 101, 107

Jupiter 7, 40, 42-45, 47

light years 10

Mars 7, 22, 36-39, 40, 104, 105
Mercury 6, 22-25, 44
meteorites 40, 61
meteoroid 60
Milky Way, the 21, 74-75, 76, 83, 84, 90
moons 6, 38, 44, 50, 56
Moon, the 18, 34-35, 58, 94

Neptune 6, 14, 54-57, 62

planets 4, 6, 7, 8, 14, 20-21, 22-33, 36-39, 42-59, 60, 61, 86-89, 96, 97, 98, 102, 104, 105
Pluto 58, 59

Saturn 7, 46-49
solar eclipses 18-19
spacecraft 80, 96, 97, 103
Space Race, the 92-95
stars 4, 8, 9, 12, 14-17, 21, 64-67, 68, 69, 70, 71, 72, 74, 85, 86, 89, 90, 98, 99
Sun, the 4, 6, 7, 14-17, 18, 22, 24, 25, 26, 28, 30, 31, 34, 40, 50, 54, 58, 62, 66, 69, 74

Uranus 7, 50-53

Venus 6, 22, 26-29